NUMBER 693

THE ENGLISH EXPERIENCE

ITS RECORD IN EARLY PRINTED BOOKS
PUBLISHED IN FACSIMILE

(THOMAS SCOTT)

SIR WALTER RAWLEIGHS GHOST, OR ENGLANDS FOREWARNER

UTRICHT, 1626

WALTER J. JOHNSON, INC.
THEATRUM ORBIS TERRARUM, LTD.
AMSTERDAM 1974 NORWOOD, N.J.

The publishers acknowledge their gratitude to
the Syndics of Cambridge University Library
for their permission to reproduce the
Library's copy, Shelfmark Syn.6.62.11 and
to the Trustees of the British Museum for their
permission to reproduce page D⁴r from
Shelfmark E.1843(5).

S.T.C. No. 22085

Collation: A-E⁴, F²

Published in 1974 by

Theatrum Orbis Terrarum, Ltd.
O.Z. Voorburgwal 85, Amsterdam

&

Walter J. Johnson, Inc.
355 Chestnut Street
Norwood, New Jersey
07648

Printed in the Netherlands

ISBN 90 221 0693 4

Library of Congress Catalog Card Number:
74-80223

SIR WALTER
RAVVLEIGHS
GHOST,

OR

Englands Forewarner.

Difcouering a fecret Confultation, newly hol-
den in the Court of Spaine.

Together, with his tormenting of Count *de
Gondomar*; and his ftrange affrightment, Confeffion
and publique recantation: laying open many
treacheries intended for the fubuer-
fion of *England*.

*Crefce, Cruor Sanguis fatietur fanguine crefce,
Quod-fpera fitio, vah fitio, fitio.*

PSAL. 14. VER. 7.
*Deftruction and vnhapineffe is in their wayes : and the
way of peace haue they not knowne, there is no feare of
God before their eyes.*

VTRICHT,
Printed by *John Schellem*
1626.

SIR WALTER RAWLEIGHS GHOST.

Lthough the liberty of thefe times (wherein your *Currants*, *Gazettas*, *Pafquils*, and the like, fwarme too too abundantly) hath made all Newes (how ferious or fubftantiall foeuer) lyable to the iealous imputation of falfhood, yet this relation I affure you (although in fome circumftances it may leane too neare the florifh of inuention, yet for the pith or marrowe thereof, it is as iuftly allyed and knit to truth, as the light is to the day, or night to darkeneffe.

To hold thee then (Gentle Reader) in no further fufpence, be pleafed to vnderftand, that fome fewe dayes after the folemnitie of the *Purification* of the bleffed Virgin (according to the Roman and Spanifh computation) It pleafed the Maieftie of *Spaine*, *Philip* the fourth, to retire himfelfe to his delicate houfe of pleafure, called *Cafa del Campo*, fituated neare vnto the towne of *Madrid* or *Madrill*, where his ftanding Court for the moft part continually remaineth: And the neareft in attendance vnto him (next to the *Cound de Oliuares*) was the *Cound de Gondomar*, the Archenemie to the florifhing Eftate of our *England*, and the Foxe whofe ftench hath not cured the *Palfey*, but rather

ther

ther impoiſoned & brought into an *Apoplexie* many Noble and ſome times well deſeruing Engliſh
hearts. Neither was the King for his pleaſure retyred to this houſe of *Pleaſure*,but rather through the
neceſſity of ſome ſpecial affaires,the greateſt wherof ſeemed to be gathered from the laſt attempt of
the Engliſh vpon the Fort & Caſtle of *Punetall* &
the town of *Cadiz* or *Cales*,wherin though the loſſe
was not ſo great or materiall as might either make
the Aſſailant or Aſſailed offer Roſes, or Nettles
vpon the Altar of Fortune; yet the affront ſeemed
to ſtrike a more deepe impreſſion in the hearts of
the Spaniards, then could be well taken away
with ſcorne (which is the enſigne of their pride)
or with the hope of future aduantage (which only
giues life vnto their *Enuie* and *Malice*.

    And therfore now at this time & in this place,after many conſultations held with the Earle of *Gondomar*, whom the whole world Baptized the *Butte
ſlaue*or *Incendiarie* of Chriſtendome,the Intelligencer, *Ambaſſadour* & *Ieſuiticall Archbiſhop Leadger* (as
his practiſes in our Nation hath well witneſſed)
touching ſome notable reuenge to be had againſt
the State of Great *Britaine*,being the onely Iewell
on which *Spaine* had long ſince fixed her heart,)to
make her vniuerſall Monarchie euery way full and
perfect,he is by command from the King (in the
perſon of the *Cound Oliuares*)to make his appearace
before the Popes *Nuntio*, the Duke of *Lerma*, the
Duke of *Cea*, the Duke of *Infantaſgo* & the Conſtable of *Caſtila*,who had a ſpeciall Comiſſion ſigned
                                                    for

for that purpofe, & to deliuer vnto them all thofe
fecret aduantages,which he had either by the experience of time,the cōtinuall labor of his braine,the
corruptiō of his bribes, the threatnings & infinua-
tiōs of his Popifh Priefts,the petulent flatteries of
his Papifticall Englifh Miftriffes dyuing into their
huʃbāds Counfels, or by any other direct or indi-
rect meanes,wonne vnto him felfe a knowledge or
inftruction for the alteration or fubuerffion of that
braue & florifhing *Britifh* Monarchie. And in this
charge the *C. de Oluares* according to the ftate and
magnificence of the Spanifh referuatiōs, began to
make a great florifh of many demure & auftere circumftances vnto the *E.* of *Gondomar*, concerning
the greatnes of his ingagemēt,the high Truft repo-
fed in his fingular knowledge, & the infinit expe-
ctations the King and the whole State had fixed
vpon the wifedom of his proceeding;adding ther-
vnto fundrie admonifhments or Caueats to call
into his remembrance, touching many alterations
in the State of Great *Britaine*, fome defenciue,
fome offenciue finee his laft aboad or comerce-
ment in the fame ; And amongft the reft as a
thing of moft efpeciall note, the *Cound* began to
repeate many relations which *Gondomar* himfelfe
had deliuered vnto him touching the generall war-
likeneffe of the *Britifh* Nation, affirming that he
had heard him fay, that he had feene the very children and boys in the ftreete, make their fport and
play a fchoole of warre,and by imitation from el-
der knowledges to expreffe in childe play, the

A 3   very

very excellencie and perfection of Martiall difcipline,which had fummoned in him both matter of
paffion & admiration,that he had often cryed out,
what will the Englifh doe,euery childe will be an Hercu-
les *and kill a Serpent in his cradle* : This,*Oliuares* tould
him was but a fmall fhadow or little pricke to expreffe a much greater fubftance now in vfe : for
fince the death of King *Iames*, of euer-liuing and
famous memorie, the Englifhmen, who for the
fpace of twenty two yeares before , had but as it
were dallyed and plaid with Armes, rather feeking
to affect it for nouelty then neceffity , were now in
one yeares deliberate and materiall exercife, become fo fingular and exquifite , that the Nether-
lands blufht to fee themfelues ouergone in a mo-
ment,& that to be made familiar in an inftat which
they had laboured to obtaine to in diuers ages.

Befides *Oliuares* affured him that he had receiued
infallible intelligece out of the Archduches Countries,that a hundred & odde of the beft experieced
fouldiers or firemen(being all *Englifh*)were fent fro
the States of the Vnited prouinces , into *Great Britaine*, to educate and inftruct in Martiall difcipline
euery feuerall Country and Prouince, in fo much
that the whole Iland was nothing now but a Nur-
cery of excellent and exquifite Souldiers.

To this *Gondomar* replyed that he had from certaine Iefuites in *England*, receiued the like intelligence,and with this addition, that thofe excellent
elected men in the Low-countries found their
equall Schoole-fellowes, nay many Tutors and
expe-

experienced Masters when they came into *England*,
so that indeed their necessitie did but conuerte to
superfluity and a little losse, to some that were of
much better deseruing.

Yet said *Gondomar* further, for mine owne part
though this make much for our terror & amazement; and that we must with *Curtius* leape wilful-
ly into a Gulphe of certaine ruine ere we can hope
of reuenge or triumphe, yet doth this new Milita-
rie courfe little moue my blood for though I must
confesse the Nether-lands to be the onely vnpara-
leld Schoole of warre in the whole world, yet the
onely thing it teacheth is *Forme* and *Fire*, *Intrench-*
ment and *Besiegement*; but for the *vse of the Sword*,
push of the Pike, *bringing of Grosses bodie to bodie and*
hand to hand, *the exercise of euery priuate strength*, *and*
the fortune of Battles, Things which the *English* must
of necessitie be expoſed vnto, *Hoc raro aut nunquam*;
And therefore (my Lord) I tell you, I more quake
when I see an old Irish Commander drilling an
English Company, who neuer beheld an enemie
but he felt his Sword and knew his Target, then
when I see infinits of golden fellows, teaching
men onely dance to the tune of *Posture*, or framing
Chimeras in their braines, whether the Pike and the
Bowe, or the Pike and Dragoone, or Pike and
long Piſtoll be of greater importance: But of
thefe things wee shall haue a larger time to difcourfe & thinke vpon, it sufficeth me that I knowe
my Royall Maſters pleaſure & your honorable in-
ſtructions; all which I will ſtudie, to ſatisfie onely
diuers

diuers things are (through other imployments,
laid as it were aside from my memory, nor vtterly
forgotten, therefore I beseech I may haue the res-
pite of some fewe houres to recken with my former knowledge, and so yeeld vp the whole summe
of my duty and seruice.

To this *Oliuares* seemed exceeding willing,& so
the Earle to make choise of his best time, they de-
parted one from the other, *Oliuares* returning to
satisfie the King,&*Gondomar* taking his Litter,went
backe to *Madrill*, where what contention grew betwixt him & his old acquainted mischieues, how
euery minute hee produced, new and vnnaturall
Cocks-egges, brooded them from the heat of his
malice,hatcht them with the deuilishnes of his *Policie*, and brought forth Serpents able to poyson
all *Europe*, is a Discourse monstrous and almost
inexpressable; I will therefore omit this mutinie
of his troubled thoughts and onely pitch vpon this
one accident, no lesse strange then memorable;
wherein as in a Mirror euery eye may behold the
weakenesse of a guilty thought, and how easily
frailty is surprised and ouercome,when it encoun-
ters with these two maine enemies of our blood,
Feare and *Amazement*.

It so fell out, that the Morning before the
Noone on which *Gondomar* was to appeare before
the designed Commissioners, partly to refresh
his perturbed spirits with the pure Ayre , and
to recollect vnto himselfe all those thoughts
and circumstances which might make a glorious
passage

paſſage for the huge and monſtrous bodie of miſchiefe where withall he was that day in labour; he cauſed his attendants to bring him in his Litter to the *Prada*, neare vnto the Cittie of *Madrill*, being a place of recreation and pleaſure for the Nobilitie and Gallantrie of Spaine, not much vnlike to our new *More field* walkes, neare to the Cittie of *London*, onely that this is more priuate and reſerued ; for as ours is common to all men of all ſorts, ſo is this *Prada* onely but for the King, the *Grandies* of Spaine, the Nobilitie and ſome Gentlemen of the vppermoſt or beſt qualitie.

After *Gondomar* had in this place of recreation taken a turne or two in his Litter, whether hee found his ruminations diſturbed with the vneaſie pace of his Mules, or that he had not elbow roome enough in his Litter, to giue action and grace to many of thoſe damnable thoughts which in that houre gaue him ſingular contentment, for the Spaniard is not of our dull Engliſh qualitie, to let his words paſſe from him as neglected ſtrangers or thoughts out of the compaſſe of his deareſt familiaritie, but rather as deare children or choiceſt friends, to lend them admiration with his eyes and hands, to adorne them with expectation in the ſhrugge of his ſhoulders, and with a thouſand other minicke geſtures, to make a ſpeech that is as triuiall and vnſeaſoned as folly it ſelfe, to appeare as ſerious as if it were a *Delphan* Oracle vpon ſome one or other of theſe Spaniſh diſguſts, this Fox (our Earle) vnkennels himſelfe and makes his

B   ſeruants

feruants take him from his Litter, then placing his chaire (the true fworne brother, or at leaft the neareft kinfman that might be to a cloffe-ftoole) vnder the fhadowe of certaine trees, in a walke more referued then the reft, he commanded his attendants to withdraw themfelues ; and he had reafon fo to doe for two principall refpects : the firft, leaft his anticke poftures, mumps, moes and Munkey-like wrye faces might drawe laughter or fcorne from his vaffals, or laftly leaft the violence of his ftudie and meditations might make fome words fall from him, which he thought too precious for another mans bofome.

Being obeyed in all his commandements, and feated thus alone by himfelfe, onely guarded by his two choife friends *Malice* and *Mifchiefe*, he had not cald vp many euill thoughts to appeare before him, when on a fodaine (according to the weakeneffe of his apprehenfion) there fhined round about him a moft glorious and extraordinary light; which might be taken rather for fire or flaming, then fhine or glittering : and this appeared fo fodainely, fpred it felfe fo largely and increafed fo violently, that terror, feare and amazement at one inftant raifd vpon the heart of the Earle, and with their colde qualities did fo ftupifie, dull and contracte all his fpirits, that as if he had feene *Medufas* head, the poore *Don* was become altogether a peece of yce or marble ; he had no fpirit to remember there were fpirits, his croffings and bleffings, his holy water and his *Agnus Dei*, his Monks charmes,

charmes, and his Iefuites coniurations were all
now turnd to quaking and trembling,to ftaring &
ftarke madnes, to gaping and groaning, to wante
of words through ftrife for words, and indeed to
what not that might fhew the fingularneffe of a
perplexed aftonifhment? his night-cap throwes
his hat in the duft, and his haire makes his cap fly
into the aire like a feather; he doth reuerence but
fees no Saint,would faine vtter either falutatiõs or
curfes,but knows not by what name to cal his controller: In the end ftarting and ftanding vpright,
feeming to fee what he would not fee, or to finde
out that with curiofitie, which he had rather loofe
with the beft care of his fpirits; ftradling like a Co-
loffes, as if he neither refpeƈted prefent perils, nor
feared thofe which were further off, he lookt as if
he would look through the pure ayre,and though
it haue truely no colour, yet was his fearche fo di-
ligent that he appeared to find out a conftant com-
plexion; yet all was but his new feare, which neither the manner of his life (which had euer beene
defperate, fubtile, and referued) the condition of
the times (at that time and in that place free from
perplexities and incumberance) the ftate of his
affaires (rather rifing then declining) nor his prefent negotiations ftrong enough to haue encoun-
tred with any *Goliahs* amazement, was able now to
keepe conftant any one ioynt about him: 1 haue
read that the Duke of *Burgundie* had like to haue
dyed at the fight of the nine Worthies, which a
Magician had difcouered but:our *Don Gondomar*

is

is like now to dye at the fight of nothing but aire
and his owne imagination; for he had euery symp-
tome of death about him, as a body trembling,
a ftomach fwelling, fore-head turnd yellow, eyes
dead or finking, a mouth gaping, & what not that
could fay our *Don* is now vpon the pitch of de-
parting. They fay that great Princes fhould neuer
fee the portraiture of feare but vpon their enemies
backes; fure I am *Gondomar* now fawe both feare
and cowardife vpon his owne heart. But why
fhould I driue you off with more circumftance?
the nakednes of the truth is, that as he gazed thus
fearefully about, there appeared or feemed to appeare before him the Ghoft of Sir *walter Ranleigh*
Knight, a Noble famous Englifh-man and a renowned Souldier: at this apparition the Earle fell
downe flat to the earth vpon his face (for backe-
ward he durft not, leaft he might giue an offence
to his Surgion) and yet the pofture in which this
Noble Gentleman appeared, how euer fearefull to
the guilte of *Gondomars* confcience, yet it was
amiable and louely to any pure and honeft compo-
fition, for he was armed at all peeces, and thofe
peeces of filuer, which is the enfigne of innocence
and harmlefneffe: In his right hand he brandifhed
his fword, which was an inftrument that had beene
euer fatall to Spanifh practifes, and had not the
edge beene taken off by this Foxes fubtilities, I
perfwade my felfe (by this time) it had neere made a
new conqueft of the Weft Indies; in his left had
he feemed to carry a cup of gold fild with blood,
which

which blood he fprinkled, fome vpon *Gondomar*
and fome vpon the ground, vttering in an hollow
and vnpleafant voyce, thefe or the like words following.

*Crefce Cruor , Sanguis fatietur fanguine Crefce, quod
fpero Sitio, ab Sitio, Sitio.*

Gondomars attendants who had all this while (a
farre off) beheld their Lords actions, feeing him
now falling downe in this trance, came with all
poffible fpeede running vnto him, but ere they
could offer an hand to his affiftance, they might
heare him vtter words of that ftrange nature and
qualitie, that their feares bridled their charities,
and they were rather willing to let him lye ftill,
bending their attëtions to his words, then by a too
officious difturbance to break off any parte of that
difcourfe which might either make for the bette-
ring of the knowledge of the State, or otherwife
be applyed to future feruice, at which thefe vnnaturall and abortiue accidents euer point, & therefore fixing their eyes and their eares conftantly
vpon him (as he lay groueling on the earth) they
might heare thefe, or like words much like vnto
thefe, proceed from his perplexed and amazed fpirit.

Bleffed foule (Noble Sir *walter Rawleigh*)what
haue I to doe with thy goodneffe, or wherefore
haft thou left the peacefulneffe of thy reft, to tor-
ment and call me to account ere the prefixed and
full day of my tryall be comed, and that I muft
ftand face to face with thee and a world of others

before

before the greateſt Tribunall, I can confeſſe mine
iniquities, and that I haue beene to the King my
maſter, as *Borgia Cæſar* was to Pope *Alexander* the
ſixt, an inſtrument willing to take vpon me any or
all manner of ſinnes how odious or vild ſoeuer, ſo
I might but make *Spaine* looke freſh, & that thoſe
imputations(which otherwiſe might haue drownd
her) might be but put into the Catalogue of my
ſeruices, though defame and curſes were heaped
vpon me, in much greater quantities then *Oſſa*,
Pelion or *Pindus*. I doe confeſſe I haue beene the very Noſe of the Spaniſh State, through which hath
beene voyded all the excrements both of the head
and the whole body: I haue beene a channell or
a Common-ſhoare to the Church of *Rome*, and
what either Pope, Prieſt, Knaue or Ieſuite could
inuent, I haue not left to put in practiſe: I knew the
odiouſneſſe of conſpiracies, and how hatefull they
are both to God and man, yet had I neuer the
power to leaue conſpiring: I knew both that the
Law of God and the law of *Honour*, tyed Princes
to deteſt conſpiracies, and had many times read
ouer that notable Hiſtorie of *Lewis* the eleuenth,
and could my ſelfe repeate the noble and famous
praiſes which all *Europe* gaue him for aduertiſing
his Arch-enemie the Duke of *Burgundie* of an attempt againſt his perſon : but what hath this
wrought in me? certes nothing but more flame
and more fuell, ſo long as my thoughts were bu-
ſied with the ſtudie and remembrance of an vniuerſall Monarchie.

I confeſſe

I confeſſe I haue many times ſaid (how euer I
haue beleeued) that thoſe great ones which ſeeke
to make away their enemies otherwiſe then by Iuſtice or the euent of warre, ſhewes minds baſe and
coward, and that their ſoules are emptie of true
courage, fearing that which they ſhould ſcorne: I
confeſſe I haue admired the goodneſſe of *Fari-
tions* who deliuered into *Pyrrhus* hand the ſlaue that
ſhould haue poyſoned him : I haue made *Tiberius
Cæſar* a demy-god, for anſwering a *King* of the
Celtes which made him an offer to poyſon *Armi-
nius, That Rome did not vſe to be reuenged of her enemies ſecretly and by deceite, but openly and by armes*;
but haue I purſued this honorable tracte : haue any
of my ghoſtly fathers the *Ieſuites*, or my maſters the
Inquiſitors giuen examples for theſe reſtrictions ?
no, their leſſons are of a cleane contrarie nature;
they ſay *Flaminius* was an honeſt man when hee
made *Pruſias* the King of *Bithinia* violate all the
lawes of hoſpitalitie and vertue, in the murther of
Haniball, but the whole *Senate* condemd the action
for moſt odious, accuſd *Flaminius* of crueltie and
coueteouſneſſe, of vaine glory and of oſtentation:
and queſtionleſſe had they had any touche or fee-
ling of Diuinitie or Chriſtianitie they could not
haue found any other ranke for him, then that next
vnto *Iudas :* theſe faire paths I haue knowne, but
theſe I haue forſaken : and as *Flaminius* was the
cauſe of *Hanibals* death out of an ambitious emu-
lation, that he might in the Hiſtories of ſucceeding
times be made notorious and eminent for ſo foule

an

an action. So I muft confeffe I that haue the whole courfe of my life labourd continually in the deep myne of pollicie; haue not fpared any blood (how excellent foeuer) fo I might be remembred in our after Annals, for one of the chiefe mafter workemen which went to the building vp of the King my mafters *Vniuerfal Monarchy:* And in this I muft confeffe, moft bleffed foul.,that thy death, thy vntimely (& to the Kingdom of Great *Britane)* much too early death(which with all violence & with all the coniurations,perfwafions &exãples that could tye & bind together the hearts and bodies of Princes, I did both plot,purfue,effect and confumate) was one of the greateft mafters peeces in which I euer triumphed ; I haue made my felfe fat with thy downefall: and the blood which iffued from thy wound , was *Nectar* and *Ambrofia* to my foule; for from thy ending I knew rightwell muft proceed *Spaines* beginning : for neuer could the Spanifh King fay as the French King did, *Ie fuis Roy feul,* I am King alone of the *Indies* as long as *Rawleigh* liued, whofe knowledge and experience was able to diuert, conuert and turne topfie turuie all his conquefts, all his proceedings. I fay the tottering ground wheron my Kings title to the *Indies* ftood, that it was nothing but violence and force, tyranie and vfurpation, and that if a ftranger or more gentle army fhould enter , how eafie it was to fet vs befides the cufhion ; this I knew thou knoweft, and what not befides which belongeth to fo great an attempt and triumphe ? I muft confeffe. I haue called

called vp into my minde the honour , the antiqui-
tie and greatneſſe of thy great Familie , how rich
thou wert in blood and friends , the whole Weſt
of the Engliſh Nation depending on thine ally-
ance : The manner of thine education , which was
not part but wholy Gentleman , wholy Souldier,
the edowments of thy vertues , which was Lear-
ning and Wiſedome ; the aduancement of thoſe
endowments , which was to be the greateſt , the
beſt , the moſt renowned Princeſſe that euer
breathed in *Europe*; and in the greateſt time of
the greateſt actions, the buſieſt time of the moſt
troubled Eſtates, the wiſeſt time for the diſcuſſion
of the moſt difficult affaires , and the onely time
that did produce the excellencie and perfection
of *wiſedome*, *warre* and *Gouernment*, ſo that nothing could be hid from thy knowledge , neither
wouldſt thou ſuffer any thing to be concealed
from thine experience, for thou hadſt euer a mind
actiuely diſpoſed; and howſoeuer thy fortune
was accompanyed with all manner of felicities,
things able in themſelues to haue drawne thy
minde from all other obiects, and to haue ſetled
thee vpon this Theorie, that ſolitarineſſe is the
moſt excellenteſt condition belonging vnto man-
kinde, in as much as in it he onely findeth the true
tranquilitie of the minde , for nothing is wanting
in that quiet habitation ; *Manna* fals there , the
Rauens bring bread from heauen ; if the waters
be bitter , there is wood to ſweeten them : If the
combate of *Amalec* & *Edom* be there, the triumphs

C   of

of *Mofes* & *Iofua* are likwiſe there, for what cannot a life rétired either ſuffer or care in its coɪtemplation; yet all this thou didſt neglect, and both contradict and diſproue: thou kneweſt this life vnfit for thy greatneſſe, and thou wert not borne for thy ſelfe but thy Countrie, thou kneweſt the Sea, wherein euery great foule ſhould wander: had no hauen but the graue, and that as they liued ſo they ought euer to dye in action. Hence it came, that euen in the very floriſh and glorie of all thy great eſtate, thou betookeſt thy ſelfe to the Seas, and what thou haſt before by thy puiſe and infinit great charge in the actions of other men wonne and annexed to the Diademe of thy great Miſtris, now thou doeſt in thine owne perſon take a vewe and ſuruay of the ſame, applying knowledge to report, and making thine owne experience a controller to other mens relations: I dare not (for the honour of my Nation) vnfolde the woefull perplexitie in which Spaine ſtood during this tedious voyage, how ſhe quaked to thinke of the generall viewe which thou hadſt taken without impeachement of all the Weſt *Indies*; but moſt of all when ſhee was aduertiſed of thy long and laborious paſſage vpon the riuer *Oranaque*, the diſtinguiſhments which thou hadſt made betwixt it and the riuer of *Amazons*; and the intelligences which thou hadſt gotten for thine aſcent to the great Cittie of *Manoa* and Kingdome of *Guyana*; deſignes which if they had beene purſued according to thy willingnes and knowledge, we

we had not at this day acknowledged one foote of
earth for ours in all the Weſt *Indies*: O the miſe-
rable eſtate of Spaine if theſe things had proceeded! ſhe had then, which now threatens all, begd
of all; and the Piſtolets of gold and peeces of plate
wherewith it now corrupts and conquers Nations, had then beene turnd to Leather or Iron,
or ſome other Spaniſh ſtuffe more baſe and con-
temptible: Was it not now high time to con-
ſpire againſt thee, to digge mine vnder-mine, to
enter into familiaritie with malcontents, to ſeduce
ſome, to bribe others, to flatter all; to preache a
thouſand moſt damnable falſe doctrines, for the
ſubuerſion of Princes and the deſtruction of their
faithfull ſeruants: was it not time for vs to make
Religion a cloake for our villanie, and vnder the
Lambs Furre to couer the Wolues policies? be-
leeue me (bleſſed ſhadow) had we either made conſcience of ſin, or ſcruples for the maintenance of
Honour, we had not ſubſiſted as we doe, but had
ſadly laine like thoſe which now lye captiued be-
low vs; can Spaine euer forget thine attempt vpon
her owne confines and in her moſt ſecureſt places,
call vp *Cadiz* to witneſſe, ſhe will ſhew you ſome
of her aſhes; call the Kings great *Armada* to account, which was led by his twelue (ſuppoſed in-
uincible Apoſtles) and the moſt of them muſt riſe
from the bottome of the ſeas, ſome muſt deſim-
bogue from your our owne harbours: Let *Pharaoh*
in *Portugall* ſpeake, and ſhe will confeſſe that her
Church will yet hardly couer her Idols. When I

looke

looke vpon the Ilands of the *Azores*, me thinkes I
fee *Fiall* burning in the flames which you caft vpon
her, whilft all the reft bring in the tributs of their
beft wealths, to faue themfelues from perifhing.
Laftly but not leaft, for from it I raifd the ground-
worke of thy fatall deftruction; I cannot but re-
count thine action vpon the Towne of St *Thoma*
ftanding vpon the riuer of *Oronoque*, how fit it lay
as a bayte to drawe thee into mifchiefe, and how
brauely it gaue me occafion neuer to defift till I
faw thy ruine; alas, was that defpifed Towne to be
prifed with thy life, with thine experience, with
thine abilitie to direct, or with the leaft parte of
thine actions? no, it was not, onely my malice
made it ineftimable, and my continuall folicita-
tions, mine imprecations, my vowes, mine ex-
clamations vpon Iuftice, mine inftances on the
actions of pious and religious Kings, and the da-
rings of too bold and ambitious Subiects, was fo
importune and violent, that but the great forfei-
ture of thy blood, my furie could finde no fatisfa-
ction : hence you fell, and that fall was to me more
then a double Banquet; for now mee thought I
faw all things fecure about me : Now faid I to my
felfe, who fhal fhake any one ftone in our building?
who fhall giue vs affright by fea, or fhew vs the
terrors of the land? what fhall hinder vs now to
bring home our gold in Caruiles, and our marchandize in Hoys and Flyboats? all is ours, the
Ocean is ours, and the *Indies* are ours : this
could wee neuer boaft before, yet this was my
                                          worke,

worke, and in this I triumphed.

At thefe words the Ghoft appeared to fhewe anger, and menacying him with frownes and the fhaking of his fword , the poore *Don* lifting vp his armes vnder his cloake, fhewd his red badge of the Order of *Colotrauia*; but finding the croffe vtterly void of vertue to diuert that charme, he began to crye out againe in this manner.

Doe not miftake me (bleffed Soule) in that I haue faid I triumphed , for I will now with griefe and repentance buy from thy mercy my abfolution. It is true that then I triumphed , for what is he that takes in hand any labor or worke of high confequence, but when he hath finifhed it to perfection , hee fits downe and reioyceth ? So I that faw (not a farre off but neare at hand) the infinite hinderances, rubs and impediments, which thy knowledge, thy valour , thy command and experience , might bring to any worke vndertaken by my King , for the aduancement or bringing forward of his vniuerfall Monarchie : and when I pondred with my felfe, that no Nation vnder heauen was fo able in power , fo apt in the nature and difpofition of the people , nor fo plentifull in all accomodations, both for fea and land, as this Iland of Great *Britaine* , to oppofe or beate backe any or all of our vndertakings, When I faw *France* bufie both at home and abroad , the Lowe-Countries carefull to keepe their owne , not curious to increafe their owne ; when I faw *Germany* afflicted with ciuill anger, *Denmarke* troubled to

C 3.   take

take trouble from his deareſt kinſman: the *Polan-der* watching of the *Turke*, and the *Turke* through former loſſes, fearefull to giue any new attempt vpon Chriſtendome, and that in all theſe we had a maine and particular intereſt: when I ſaw euery way ſmooth for vs to paſſe, and that nothing could keepe the Garland from our heads, or the Goale from our purchaſe but onely the anger or diſcontent of this fortunate Britiſh Iland; blame me not then if I fell to practiſes vnlawfull, to flat-teries deceitfull, to briberie moſt hurtefull, and to other enchantments moſt ſhamefull, by which I might either winne mine owne ends, or make my worke proſperous in the opinion of my Soue-raigne. I confeſſe I haue many times abuſed the Maieſtie of Great *Britaine* with curious falſhoods, I haue proteſted againſt my knowledge, and vtte-red vowes and promiſes which I knew could neuer be reconciled: I haue made delayes, ſharpe ſpurs to haſten on mine owne purpoſes, & haue brought the ſwifteſt deſignes to ſo ſlowe a pace, that they haue beene loſt like ſhadowes, and neither known nor regarded: I lookt into your Common-wealth, and ſaw that two and twenty yeares eaſe had made her grow idle; I ſaw the Eaſt *Indies* eate vp and de-uoure your Mariners & Sea-men, & time and old age conſume and take away your land Captaines; and of all, none more materiall then your ſelfe: Blame me not then if I made thine end my begin-ning, thy fall the fulneſſe of my perfection, and thy deſtruction the laſt worke or maſter-peece of

all

all my wifedome and pollicie. This is the free-
dome of my confeffion, and but from this finne
abfolue me, and I will dye thy penitent in facke-
cloath and afhes.

At thefe words the apparition feemed (in the
fearefull imagination of the poore *Don*) to be
more then exceeding angrie, and lookt vpon him
with fuch terror and amazement, that *Gondomar*
fell (with the affright) into a trance or deadly
found, whileft the Ghoft feemed to vtter vnto
him thefe or thefe like words following.

To thee whom bafe flatterie, wante and coue-
teoufneffe hath guilded with thefe foolifh and vn-
fitting hyperboles, as to call thee,

The Flower of the Weft,
The delight of Spaine,
The life of Wit.
The light of Wifedome.
The Mercurie of Eloquence.
The glorie of the Gowne.
The Phebus in Court.
Neftor *in Counfell.*
Chriftian Numa,
and principall ornament of this time.

    Lord Diego Sarmiento de Acuna, Moft honorable
Earle of Gondomar, *Gouernour of* Menroyo, *and*
Pennarogo, *of the moft honorable Order of* Colatra-
uia, *Counfellour of State, one of the Kings Treafurers,*
Embaffadour for his Catholicke Maieftie to his Royall
Maieftie of England, Regent of the Towne and Caftle of
Bayon, *Prefident of the Bifhopricke of* Tuid *in* Ga-
litia,

litia, *Chiefe Treasurer of the most noble Order of* Alcantara, *One of the foure Iudges of the sacred Priuiledges*, *Pronotarie of the Kingdome of* Toledo, Leon
and Galitia, *and Principalitie of* Astures, *And Lord
high Steward of the most Puissant*, Philip *the IIII.
King of all the* Spaines *and of the* Indies.

Loe thus I salute thee with thy true Stile and
eminent Inscription according to thine absolute
Nature, Qualitie and Profession;

To thee then that art,

The poysonous weed of Europe.

The Atlas of Spaines *sinnes and conspiracies.*

The Deuils foole.

The Wisemans Bugbeare.

Gondomars
true Title or
Stile.
The Mercurie *of knauish Policie.*

The disgrace of Ciuilitie.

The Buffoone in Courte.

Ate in Counsell.

*Atheist, for the Popes aduantage, and principall In-
telligencer betweene Hell and the Iesuites.*

Don Diego Sarmiento de Acuna; *Most dishonorable
Earle of* Gondomar, *Pouller and Piller of* Menroyo,
and Pennaroyo, *of the riche couetous Order of* Co-
latrauia, *Gazetist of State, one of the consumers of
the Kings purse, Intelligencer for his Catholicke Maiestie against the Royall Maiestie of* England, *Spoiler of
the Towne and Castle of* Bayon, *an ill example to the
Bishopricke of* Tuid *in* Galitia, *Chiefe cash-keeper
for the Order of* Alcantara, *One of the foure Bribe-ta-
kers for the prophane priuiledges, Promoter for the
Kingdome of* Toledo, Leon *and* Galitia, *and Principalitie*

cipalitie of **Aſtures**, *and a continuall Broker betweene the King of* Spaine *and the Pope, and betweene the* Ie-ſuites, *the* Inquiſitors *and the Deuill.*

Harken to my detection, and though I knowe thou canſt ſteale and kill, ſweare and lye, weepe and wound, and indeed doe any thing that is con-trarie to Truth and Iuſtice; yet in this accuſation, ſhame and thine owne putrified conſcience ſhall be witneſſes ſo powerfull and vndaunted, that thou ſhalt not be able to refell any one allegation or ſmalleſt particle.

To begin then with mine owne end, though I know the day of my death was the greateſt Feſti-uall that euer thy fortune did ſolemnize, though it brought to *Spaine* a yeare of *Iubile*, to thy repu-tation *Abſolans* pillars, and to euery Papiſticall Miniſter in the world, the praiſe of his Arteſ-ma-ſter; yet poore deſpiſed mortall, know, it was not you, but a more diuine and inſcrutable finger which pointed out my deſtinie to this manner of end & deſtruction, neither is it fit for the humility of ignorant man to open his eyes, as daring to pre-ſume to gaze on the radiant beames of that ſoue-raigne power, which diſpoſeth of ſecōdcauſes as he pleaſeth: neither doe I afflict thee as my particular executioner, but as my Countries generall enemy: It ſufficeth me that the great God who is Iudge of life & death, hath diſpoſed of my life, & after this early manner, that in it he might expres the effects of his Iuſtice; therefore trouble not thy ſelfe with my death which was thy comfort, but be vexed at

D   thine

thine owne life, which is nothing but a continuall
pilgrimage to Ambition, and an vndermining
Moale to digge downe the Chruch of God, and
to bring the Gofpell of our bleffed Sauiour into
eternall captiuitie. Haft not thou beene an vnti-
red packe-horfe, trauelling night and day without a baite, and loaden like ad Affe, till thy
knees haue bowed vnder the burthen of ftrange
and vnnaturall defignes, by which to aduance
thy Mafter to the vniuerfall Monarchie of all Europe ? This thy feare hath made thee confeffe, but
this thy flatterie and falfhood will deny, fhould
not the efficacie of truth make it moft apparant
and pregnant : Therefore to enter into the firft
ftreames from whence Spaine hath gathered the
great Ocean of its Soueraigntie, there is no foun-
taine more remarkable then the Battle of Alcazar
in Barbarie, where the too forward Don Sebaftian
King of Portugall (whether flaine or not flaine) in-
gaging himfelfe too vnfortunately, gaue occafion to Philip the fecond of Spaine, to enter and
vfurpe vpon his kinfmans Kingdomes, to expell
Don Antonio from his right and inheritance, and
as it is ftrongly fuppofed, to caufe the true King
himfelfe to dye in the Gallies; hence he became
King of all the Spaines and Portugall, puld to himfelfe the Soueraignetie both of the Ilands of the
Canaries and of the Azores, the one fecuring his
way forth, the other fecuring his way home from
the Weft Indies, and fo made the conqueft thereof
more fafe and vndoubded : hee tooke alfo by the
                                         fame

same interest many strong holds & marchantable
places in the East *Indies*, so that sitting now alone
in *Spaine* without a competitor, and hauing treasure from the West *Indies* wherewith to pay Souldiers, and marchandize from the East *Indies* wher-
with to enrich his owne subiects, what could he,
or what did hee contemplate vpon but the aug-
mentation of his Monarchie : Hence it came that
his warre grewe violent vpon the Low-Countries
and vnder the Gouernments of the Duke of *Alua*,
and *Don Iohn* Duke of *Austria*, the tyrannies so in-
sufferable, that all manner of freedomes were con-
uerted to slaueries, and the blood of the Nobilitie made only foode for the slaughter-house, yea
such as were remote and stood farther off from
his crueltie, depending vpon their owne rights
and vnder the couert of their owne guards, were
not yet safe from *Spaines* conspiracies, and that
witnesseth the death and murther of the famous
Prince of *Orange*, the imprisonment and death of
his eldest sonne, and a world of infamous practises against the life of Count *Maurice*, the last
Prince deceased, and against the safetie of Count
Henrike the Prince now suruiuing : what incroch-
ments were daily made vpon these distressed Prouinces, all the Princes of *Europe* blush to behold,
and had not *Elizabeth* my dread Ladie and Mistris
of famous and blessed memorie, taken them to
her Royall protection, they had long since beene
swallowed vp in the gulphe of his tyrannie, and
none of them now liuing had knowne the name of

D 2   free

free Princes: and as this worke was begun by *Philip* the second, so it was continued by *Philip* the third, and is now at this houre as earnestly pursued by *Philip* the fourth and his sister the Archduchesse, and rather with gaining then loosing; so that should *England* but turne its face a little away from their succour, there would be a great breache made in the hope of their subsisting.

But you will answere, that if *Spaine* had fixed down its resolution vpon an vniuersall Monarchy, they had neuer then harkned to a peace with the Nether-Lands: to this thine owne conscience is ten thousand witnesses, that the peace which it entertained, was nothing else but a politicke delay to bring other and imperfit ends and designes, to a more fit and solid purpose, for effecting of his generall conquest: for what did this Truce, but diuert the eyes of the Nether-lands (which at that time were growing to be infinit great masters of shipping) from taking a suruay of his *Indies*, and brought a securitie to the transportation of his plate and treasure, and made him settle and reinforce his Garrisons which then were growne weake and ouertoyled, besides a world of other aduantages, which too plainely discouered themselues assoone as the warre was new commenced.

As he had thus gotten his feete into the Netherlands, had not *Spaine* in the same manner, and with as much vsurpation, thrust his whole body into *Italy?* let *Naples* speake, let *Sicill,* let the Ilands
of

of *Sardinia* and *Corfica*, the Dukedome of *Millan*, the reuolte of the *Valtoline* and a world of other places, fome poffeft , fome lying vnder the pretence of ftrange Titles, but come to giue vp their account, and it will be more then manifeft , that no Signorie in all *Italie* but ftood vpon his guard, and howerly expected when the Spanifh ftorme fhould fall vpon them ; how many quarrels hath beene piled againft the State of *Venice*, fome by the *Pope*, fome by the King of *Spaine* ? how many doubts haue beene throwne vpon *Tufcanie*? what proteftations haue flowne to *Genoa* , and what threatnings againft *Geneua* ? and all to put *Italy* into conbuftion, whilft the *Popes* holineffe , and his Catholicke Maieftie , like *Saturnes* fonnes , fat full gordgd with expectation to deuide heauen and earth betweene them.

O was it not a braue politicke tricke of *Spaine*, (neither was thine aduice abfent from the mifchiefe) when the difference fell betweene *Henry* the Great of *France* and the Duke of *Sauoye* , about the Marquifate of *Salufes*; the King then your mafter vnder pretence of aiding the Duke his brother in Law , fent diuers Regiments of Spaniards which were quartered fome in *Carbonieres*, fome in *Montemellion*, *Sauillan* , *Pignoroll* and diuers other places about *Sauoye* and *Piemont* , but when the Truce was concluded , could the Duke vpon any intreatie , potent or meffage make thefe Spaniards to quit his Countrie? no, by no meanes, for they were fo farre from leauing their foot-hold,

hauing,

hauing receiued diuers commandments to keepe
it, both from the Count *de Fuentes* (at that time
Vice-roy of *Millan*) from thee by priuate letters,
and from the King your Mafter by fundrie Com-
miffions; that the chiefes of thofe Troopes, pe-
remptorily anfwered the Duke, that they would
hould their gettings, in defpight of all oppofi-
tions, and were indeed full as good as their words
for a long time, till at laft the Duke (inforced
thereunto) raifed vp a ftrong Army, and in a fewe
dayes put them all to the fword, I would here repeate the Spanifh attempt againft the Caftle of
Nice, being the very key or opener of an entrance
into the very bowels of *Italie*; I could fpeake of
the dangerous quarrel raifd betweene the Duke of
Sauoye and the Duke of *Mantoa*, for the Marquifate of *Montferrat*, and how fatall it was likely to
haue beene to the whole ftate of *Italy*, wherein
Fuentes and thy felfe, fhewd all the arte of practife
that might be, which, fhould become the mafter
worke-man; but thefe things are fo pregnant and
apparant that they neede little difcuffion.

Let mee now awaken thy memory with fome
ftirrings vp or practifes againft the Kingdome of
France, no leffe but more pernitious then any of
the former; who was the head or chiefe foueraigne
(after the the death of *Henry* the third King of
France and *Poland*) of that moft vnchriftianlike
combination, intituled the *Holy*, but truely *vn-
holy League*? was it not *Philip* of *Spaine* one of your
moft Catholike Mafters, who made the great and
valiant

valiant *Guife* his fword and feruaut, the ould
Queene mother his intelligencer and admirer,
the Cardinals his Minifters and feducers, and the
Pope himfelfe a Prodigall childe, to beftow and
giue away whatfoeuer hee required? was not all
this *Philip* of *Spaine* your Catholike Mafter? How
long did he keepe *Henry* the fourth furnamed the
Great, from his lawfull Throne and inheritance?
what Citties did hee poffeffe? euen the greateft
that *France* could number: what Countries vnder
his command? all that were rich or fruitfull: and
what Nobilitie had hee drawne from their obedience? thofe that were more powerfull and beft
beloued; in fo much, that had not my moft excellent Miftris *Elizabeth*, of bleffed and famous Memory, like a ftrong Rocke againft the rage of a
furious fea, taken the qnarrell into her hand, and
by her Royall protection, firft vnder the conduct
of the Lord *Willoughby*, after vnder the conduct of
the Earle of *Effex*, ftaid and fupported that ree-
ling Eftate, *France* it is feared, at this houre had
onely fpoken the Spanifh language: but God in
his great mercie had otherwife difpofed of thefe
practifes, and though with fome difficulties,
brought the Crowne of *France* to its true owner;
a Prince fo abfolutely excellent in euery perfection of true honour and magnimitie, that his pa-
ralell hath not beene found in all the Hiftorie of
France, and although hee had in his very youth
and almoft child-hood preuailed in diuers Battles,
as that at *Montconter*, and at *Rene-le.duke*; and
                                                    although

although hee had beene affayled in the dayes of
Henry the third, and in the fpace of foure yeares,
by ten Royall Armies fucceffiuely one after another, and fent one to refrefh the other, and vnder
the conduct of great and moft glorious Captaines, againft all which he preuailed, as witnef-
fed his victorie at the Battle of *Contras* and other
places, though he had giuen fuccour to *Henry* the
third, and deliuered him from his great danger
at *Tours*, bringing to his obedience *Gargeau*, *Gien*,
la Charite, *Pluuiers*, *Eftampes*, *Dourdan* and diuers
other places : though hee had beene generally
fortunate in all his great actions, yet after the
death of *Henry* the third, this deuillifh combination, or Spanifh knot of the *League* is more omi-
nous, fatall and troublefome vnto him, then all
his former vndertakings; and hee found that although hee might haue come to the Crowne of
France by fucceffion, which was the eafieft way,
yet God to trie his courage, to exercife the force
of his minde, and to make a foolifh fhadowe or
Ignis Fatuus of *Spaines* Ambition, prefented the
moft painefull and difficult vnto him, which was
that of Conqueft : Hee was forft to raife on foote
(by the helpe of our Englifh Nation) three Royall
Armies, which he difperft in three Prouinces; the
firft, into *Normandie*, where he was affifted by the
Earle of *Effex*, the fecond into *Champaigne*, and
the third into *Picardie*, where hee was feconded
by the Lord *willoughbie*, who brought him trium-
phantly into the fuburbs of *Paris*, and by the
blowing

blowing vp of a Porte, offerd to deliuer the whole
Cittie to his fubiection ; the Earle of *Effex* did as
much at *Roan* , but the King defired to winne
France, not to deftroy *France* , yet ere the Earle de-
parted, he chafed rebellion out of the moft part
of *Normandie* : the King gaue his enemis (the Spanifh faction) battle vpon the plaine of *Yury* and
wonne it , by which he regained in leffe then two
months fifteene or fixteene great Townes, brought
Paris to infinit extreamitie , made the Spaniards
wifh themfelues on the other fide of the *P reneans:*
and indeede fuch a generall amazement to all the
vnhappie *Leaguers* , that all ftood agaft , as vncer-
taine which way to turne them.

This when your great Mafter beheld , and faw
that all his hopes were dying in an inftant , like a
cunning Coniurer hee feekes to drawe fire and
lightning from heauen, to confume what his Armies durft not approach or difualewe , whence it
came, that he roufes vp *Gregorie* the 13. then Pope,
who indeed was the O.acle, or rather the creature of *Philip* your mafter , and makes him of a
common Father betweene the head of a rebel-
lious and vfurping partie , cafting forth his fulmi-
nations with fuch violence and iniuftice , that the
Buls were taken and burnt both at *Tours* and at
Chalons ; neither fent he out thefe Buls by his vn-
godly and bloodie Minifters the Iefuites , or fuch
like defperate and obfcure mal-contents , but with
an Army of a thoufand caffacks of watchet veluet,
imbrodred with gold, and Ciphers of Keys ioyned

E   vnto

vnto fwords (whofe errand was, to demand the
execution of thefe Buls) now feing the difficultie
wherein affaires flood, vpon the vew of one hundred horfe of the French Kings white Cornet,
dare not for all the Pope or the King of *Spaines*
hopes or commandements abandon the very fhadowe of the walles of *Verdun*, but like fo many
Foxes lay lurking in their kennels of fecurity,
knowing they had to deale with mē, whofe fwords
were fo well fteeld, that they feared not the lead
of *Rome*, onely like fo many Furies of hell they
feeke to breake all treaties of peace, and made it an
action treafonable and moft impious, to talke of
an vnity betweene the Soueraigne and the fub-
ict.

But for all this, great *Henry* loft no time, for
firft, he paffed into *Normandy*, fecured his friends
there, thence hee went into *Picardie*, befieged
Noyon and tooke it, euen in the view of the Spanifh Armie, who although they were three to
one, yet durft not to hazard the Battle : which
aduantage the King wifely taking, and turning
head vpon his enemies, albeit hee was aduifed to
the contrary by his chiefeft feruants, yet his courage bound him rather to follow the path of danger with honour, then that of fafety with fhame,
faying as *Pompey* faid, *That in ftriking his foot againft
the earth he would raife vp Legions:* fo the Armies
met together at *Aumale*, where though vpon the
firft approach the King was hurt with a fhot, yet
he had ftrength enough to crye *Charge, Charge*, and
breaking

breaking through his enemies, he put the Duke of
Parma and all his Spaniards to a fhamefull re-
traite; as this, fo he beat his enemies at *Bellencombe*,
he ftripes them at *Bure*, and made them to quit
Yuetot with much fhame and loffe.

Thus this Royall Kings quarrell being iuft, and
maintained by a good fword, the pride of *Spaine*
found that if the warre contained longer, her Catholike grea-neffe, could haue more wood to heat
her Ouen, then corne to fend to the Mill.

Tis purpofeleffe to fpeake of the ruine of
Quibeuf, the recouerie of *Efpernay*, or that braue
affault, where eight Horfes put three hundred to
route; let it fuffice me in one word to conclude,
that in defpight of all the engines which the Pope
or the King of *Spaine* could vfe, *Henry* of *France*
became triumphant, and your Mafters vniuerfall
Monarchie was turnd topfie turuie; nay, the
League the *Typhon* of fedition from whence fprung
fo many Serpents and Vipers of difloyalty, was
fmothered vnder the *AEtna* of her owne prefum-
ption and pride.

But did either *Spaine* or *Rome* here ftay their malice? fie no, but rather *Anteus* like, they rofe vp
with double vigor, and what publique warre
could not effect, priuate practife and confpiracie
muft bring to paffe, for ere the Great *Henry* was
well warmed in his Throne, *Hell* and the Spanifh
gold ftird vp a wretch, who vndertooke to kill
him; the Tyger ftaid his hand at the fhining of a
glaffe, and after his apprehenfion, confeft that hee

fawe

fawe fo much pietie and zeale fhining in the eyes
of this Prince, that he felt horrour in himfelfe to
offend the Soueraigne dignity ordained of God
among Angels and Men. Hence it came that all
France beheld and tooke notice of *spaines* Ambition, & that indeed all their labour was but to re-
duce that florifhing Nation to a priuate Prouince,
which the Parliament of *Paris* (after it had vomi-
ted the phlegme of temporizing) taking to heart,
made forth a Decree for the difperfing and ba-
nifhing of all the Spanifh Regiments : and now
fiue great Dukes, formerly bewitched with Catholike incantations, fall at the foote of this
great King, and confeffe how they were beguy-
led.

The firft, was the Duke of *Lorraine*, which ob-
tained a generall Peace for his Eftate, through
the mediation of *Ferdinand* the Archduke of *Tufcanie* ; the fecond was the Duke of *Mayenna*,
who abtained pardon through the wifedome of
his carryage, hauing ftill a watchfull eye, that no
generall ruine might happen to the Kingdome;
The third, was the Duke of *Guife*, the loffe of
whofe father and vnckle, made his intereft the greateft in this quarrell, yet had he the honour to receiue the Kings firft imbraces ; The fourth was the
Duke of *Ioyeufe*, who as foone as hee had kift the
Kings hand, forfooke the troubles of the world,
betooke himfelfe to a folitary life ; and the laft was
the Duke *Mercure*, who brought to the King, not
himfelfe alone, but with him the reduction of the
good-

goodlyeſt Prouince in all *France* : To conclude
Philip of *Spaine* your Maſter , ſeing vpon what falſe
wheeles his engins ranne , was content to intreate
for peace of this great Cheiftaine.

But did here conſpiracies and Spaniſh plots
end ? no , nothing ſo : for to come nearer to your
owne touche , and to repeate matters of thine
owne proſecution , Is it not an Hiſtorie moſt remarkable , and to *Spaine* moſt infamous , of that
deſperate vilaine borne at *Negre-peliſſe* , who
going into *Spaine* vpon ſome diſcontents concei-
ued againſt this great *Henry* of *Frauce*, and as it
was ſtrongly ſuppoſed , hauing taken ſome dire-
ctions from you , but full and materiall inſtru-
ctions from the Deuils poſt horſes your maſters
the Ieſuites , did with all violence proſtitute himſelfe to murther this moſt Chriſtian King ; but the
matter being ſo important , and carryed through
ſo many ſeuerall hands , had loſt ſo much ſtreng h
of ſecrecie , that an inckling thereof came to the
eares of *de Barraut*, then ordinarie Ambaſſadour in
Spaine for the King of *France* , who inſtantly out
of dutie , and the hatred which euery true Chriſtian ought to beare againſt theſe odious and moſt
Atheiſticall practiſes , complained to the Popes
Nuntio, hoping of redreſſe , both againſt the vilaine himſelfe , your ſelfe and the Ieſuites , who
are both vilaines and your ſelfe ; but the matter
was fully blancht , and your impious care (that
had liſtned to this abhominable ſinne) was excu-
ſed , and the whole offence of ſubornation was
laid

laid vpon a creature of yours; but one of the King
of *Spaines* Efquiers , named by the place of his
birth *Valdomoro* , who vpon examination (hauing
his leſſon fore-taught him , confeſt all the paſſa-
ges to the Duke of *Lerma*, and that not onely this
ſlaue, but diuers others had tendred themſelues to
the like ſeruice , yet this with the greateſt violence, aſſuring him that he knew the meanes how
to kill the King ; which propoſition , vpon ſome
conference with a Ieſuite(who neuer take diſtaſt at
ſuch a practiſe) he had accepted of, but yet with
that caution and delay that nothing proceeded
therein , neither was likely to proceed , and ſo all
things were ſhut vp without any further diſcoue-
rie , onely that *de Barraut* aduertiſed the King his
Maſter thereof : but was this honorable or pious
in *Spaine*? no , the praiſe had beene more perfect,
and the merit more plaine and euident for the
Spaniards , if they had puniſhed the Traytor,
made thy ſelfe *Valdomoro* , and the Ieſuite examples,not to liſten or giue eare to ſuch odious conſpiracies , and by a carefull aduertiſement to the
King , made others dread the entering into ſo
odious a buſineſſe ; for it is true in all the lawes of
hoſpitalitie , that this ſlaue ought not to haue
come out of *Spaine* vnchaſtiſed , for all Kings are
brothers , and all Kingdomes intereſſed in theſe
attemps. But the deſignes of *Spaine* lookt now an
other way , and the Traytor had leaue to eſcape,
who returning afterwards into *France* , was by *de*
Verdun firſt Preſident of *Languedoc* , apprehended
at

at *Tholouse* and there executed, and his companion condemnd to the Gallies. O how farre was this action shorte, of that Royall and Princely acte of the famous late Queene *Elizabeth*! who hauing receiued intelligence of some Spanish mischieues pretended against this great King, forthwith gaue him intelligence, that a strange Gentleman, who was one of his followers, had no good meaning towards his person, and related vnto him euery circumstace as she had receiued it; but such was the bountie of this great King, that allbe reason would that he should haue bin apprehended, yet the King neuer discouered vnto him a frowne, but he still remained in the Court well entertained, was mounted out of the Kings stable, and honoured with many of his trustie comandements, till in the end torturd with his owne conscience, he stole away from the Court, & durst no longer abuse so Royall a bountie; that this was a Fauorite of *Spaine* your selfe cannot deny, that he fled from *France* into *Spaine*, your one Cabanet is a witnesse, and that you did preserue him for the like exploits in others places : the marke on his face, the colour of his beard, and his cloaths cut after the *walloone* fashion were too apparant testimonies.

I might here recounte this great Kings death by *Rauiliac*, from whose blood, neither thy selfe nor *Spaine* can wash themselues, though all the Riuers in the world were exhausted and thrust into one entyer Bath, and so spent vpon your particular
lar

lar cleanfings ; but thefe truths are fo frefh in memorie, they need neither repeating , nor ampli-
fica ion.

I could to thefe adde a world of others , as the
attempts vpon the life and fafety of the late
Queene *Elizabeth* of famous memorie, and the
making of all thofe inhumane creatures Pentio-
ners of *Spaine* , who had either by rebellion or
other treafonable practife , attempted any thing
for her vntimely and fad deftruction.

Was our late dread Souera gne, King *Iames*
of bleffed and happy memorie, that *Salomon* of his
time , a Prince fo indulgent and carefull for euery
good thing that might happen to *Spaine* , a man fo
tender and vigilant for her reputation , that hee
euer plac'd it in the next rancke to his owne honour ? was he I fay ? was this good King free from
the bloody practifes of *Spaine* ? no , to the eternall
infamie of ingratefull and bloody *Spaine* : I may
euer proclaime it that he was more deepely plun-
ged and his like, more bitterly befieged and af-
faulted, then any whatfoeuer before rehearfed:and
to this I call vp the plot of all plots, that Deuill
of many legions of Deuils ,the Gun-pouder confpiracie, that which fhould haue deftroyed all,
not a fingle Princ or a fingle man , but many
Princes , many mens whole generations; here
was cruell *Spaine* and here indeed (had not God
preuented was a ftrong foundation for an vniuerfall Monarchie; and that *Spaine* may not in this,
pleade not guilty : let her difcouer to the world
what

what occurrents they were which drew *Thomas winter* into her confines, what negotiation was that which hee held with *de Laxis*, whence came his inftructions and letters commendatorie into the Archducheffe Countrie? where did *Guy Faucks* receiue his breeding? who gaue information of his knowledge in myning? and who preferred and aduanceft him to this peece of moft damnable feruice? queftionleffe let truth anfwere to any of thefe pofitions, and the fpeech it muft vtter, will be Spanifh language; who in all this Nation was fo intimate with you as the Archprieft *Garnet*? or who like him found at your hands equall prote- ction? he confeft and abfolued the Traytors, and thou didft abfolue and confeffe him, and thereby didft get vnto thy felfe from thine owne Tribe, the nicke-name of *Archbifhop Ambaffadour*.

Thus I haue brought *Spaines* attempsfor an vni- uerfall Monarchie, from *Portugall* to the *Nether- lands*, thence through *Italy*, fo into *France*; En- g*land* was lookt vpon by the way, in the yeare 1588. but fhee was not fo drowfie as others: there is now but *Germanie* betwixt him and the end of his Ambition, but is that free and vntouched? woe to fpeake it, that of all is the worft and moft horred: O the lamentable eftate, of thofe once moft happie Princes! how hath the houfe of *Au- ftria* drownd them in blood? and by the worke of ciuill diffention, made them in their furies to de- uoure one another. Is there any thing in this age more lamentable or remarquable, then the loffe

F   of

of the *Palatinate*? or is there any thing in which
thy villany can so much triumph as in that poli-
tique defeature? why, the lyes which thou didst
vtter to abuse the Maiestie of *England*, and to
breed delayes till thy Masters designes were effe-
cted, were so curious and so cunning, so apte to
catch, and so strong in the holding, that the Deuill (who was formerly the author of lyes) hath
now from thee taken new presidents for lying. I
would here speake of thy Archduchesses dissimu-
lation, but shee is a great Lady, and their errours
at the worst are weake vertues.

Therefore to thee that hast lent both fuell and
flame to all the mischiefes of *Europe*, and that art
now bigge in labour with new troubles and vexa-
tions, arise and collect thy spirits, become once
honest and religious, let thy seruices depend
vpon good and necessarie affaires, and not vpon
malicious and bloody practises: for behold, I
thy *Tormentor* will neuer be absent from thine elbow, and whatsoeuer thou shalt contriue or plot
for the hurt of Great *Britaine*, I with the helpe of
the holy Angels will returne vpon thine owne bosome and the bosome of thy Countrie, for the
good of heauen and earth, who is the Protector
of the Innocent; hath made Royall King
C H A R L E s and his Throne precious in his sight,
therefore if thou desirest to liue and see good
dayes, touch not his annointed and doe his *Pro-
phets* no hurt.

At these words, the glorious aparition (wauing
his

his fword about) vanifhed out of his fight,
and the poore *Don* as if awakened from a deadly
or mortall fleepe rofe vp , looking about with
fuch gaftly amazedneffe as affrighted all that beheld him. In the end efpying his owne feruants,
with teares in his eyes, terrour in his heart , and a
generall trembling ouer all his body , he went into his Litter , and returned home, where how
he refrefht himfelfe , how hee appeared before the
defigned Commiffioners , and how he anfwered
the expectation both of them and the King his
Mafter,fhall be declared vpon the next returne
of the woman Pofte which paffeth betwixt the Englifh and the
Spanifh *Iefuits.*

F I N IS.